SALES SCRIPT YOU WILL FIND IN THIS BOOK ...

I used this script on my sales calls, and by the third week, I went from selling $1,000 monthly retainers to $30,000 packages.

—**Tom Camp,** TomCampConsulting.com

I used this sales script to close the first sales call I ever took. I was nervous as hell until I heard that first "YES" and knew this worked. Fast forward to today, I've generated $1.6M in my business. This script slays.

—**Carl Parnell,** CarlParnell.co

At our office, we call Dan's script the "Rolls Royce Method to closing High Ticket," and here is why: Rolls Royce is known for dialed-in engineering, so their vehicles run perfectly. With such detail and effort, why wouldn't you use the best tactics and strategy from an expert who has truly created a masterpiece? We have used Dan's script to go from struggling to hit $30,000 per month, to now having multiple 6-figure months, to bringing in millions per year.

Michael Fomkin, VIPignite.com

We used Dan's script to increase sales by 410% over the past year. It's literally like taking candy from a baby.

—**Ken Underhill,** CyberLife.TV

I used this script to go from broke music producer to making my annual income on a monthly basis now. This is truly the best thing you can do for yourself if you like money!

—**Christopher To,** ProduceBeatsArtistsBuy.com

When I started my dating coaching business, I was a broke student living in tiny student housing without any sales experience. I studied Dan's sales script, and on the third call I ever took, I closed my first HT sale of €3k. After that, I consistently closed HT sales, which allowed me to quit my study and travel full time all over the world. Now that I've used it to build a business with a proper team, I also have complete time freedom. It honestly changed my life forever.

—**Rick Smits,** VIPdatingconsulting.com

I used Dan's sales script for my local service business and went from "convincing" people to buy $3K packages to regularly closing $8 to $10K deals, and my typical sales call is less than 20 minutes.

—**Nick Keesey,** 90dayBusinessMastery.com

Hands down one of the best sales scripts we have ever used. This framework took our company's annual revenue from $100K to over $400K in less than 12 months! It's better than money—it gives you the ability to print it on demand!

—**Zachary J. Radford,** ProfitableAds.com

THE POCKET GUIDE TO HIGH TICKET SELLING

A 12-PHASE SALES SCRIPT YOU CAN USE TO SELL MILLIONS OVER THE PHONE

DAN HENRY

THE POCKET GUIDE TO HIGH TICKET SELLING

A 12-Phase Sales Script You Can Use to Sell Millions Over the Phone

For permission requests, speaking inquiries, and bulk order purchase options, email business@closedeals.com.

CloseDeals.com

ISBN: 978-1-7344284-1-4

Cover and Interior Design by Transcendent Publishing
transcendentpublishing.com

Edited by Lori Lynn Enterprises

Printed in the United States of America.

“

EVERYTHING in life is a sale.

From selling yourself to a potential romantic partner, to selling your kids on eating their vegetables, to selling someone on working for you, all the way to selling your products.

EVERYTHING is a sale.

The sooner you learn to sell, the better your life will be.

—**Dan Henry,** *WSJ & USA Today* bestselling author of *Digital Millionaire Secrets*

60-SECOND SALES TIPS

If you purchased this book on Amazon instead of through our website, you may not be receiving our **60-Second Sales Tip Newsletter**. Every day, we send out a short sales or marketing tip. We know you're busy, so each tip only takes 60 seconds to consume. You can sign up for the sales tips newsletter at:

CloseDeals.com/60seconds

A WORD OF THANKS

First and foremost, I want to thank all of the customers over the years who have heard the words *you'll learn inside this book* … and, as a result, bought my products. Even more so, I'd like to thank the customers who not only learned the script found in this book, but also took action and used what they learned to make their dreams come true.

Second, I'd like to thank my partner and COO at CloseDeals.com, Phil Bohol, for not only contributing to this book but also completely taking the burden of running the company and managing employees off of my shoulders. Because of him, I was able to hang out in Costa Rica and write this book for a full week and do nothing else. If it wasn't for him, I'd get nothing done.

I'd also like to thank my team who, with Phil at the helm, make all the crazy and wacky ideas that I come up with in my head make sense. Everything I throw in their direction in a chaotic tornado, they manage to implement so our company can grow. I also want to give a special shout-out to our sales pros who execute this content every day. None of this would be possible without them.

I also want to thank Lori Lynn, who is the best book editor I've ever met. She was gracious enough to edit this book at the 11th hour. She did a fantastic job, just like she did with my last book, *Digital Millionaire Secrets.* If you're an author, you'd be a fool not to hire her.

I'd like to thank Shanda Trofe for being an absolute rockstar designer and getting this book formatted and published, again, at the 11th hour, as she does with most of my wacky ideas. This is yet another extremely talented person that anyone would be crazy not to hire.

I'd also like to thank my mentors, sales managers, and all the people I've learned sales from over the years who have contributed to me even being in the position to write such a book. This includes Myron Golden, Sam Ovens, Kevin Nations, Ryan Stewman, and many others. There are so many that I couldn't possibly mention them all.

And finally, my son Bruce, who is a continual source of inspiration for me. Being his dad motivates me to improve as an entrepreneur so I can teach him the ways of the business world and as a father so I may show him a path to becoming a better man than I am. I know you can't read yet, but when you can, make sure you read this book, son.

TABLE OF CONTENTS

FOLLOW DAN ON SOCIAL FOR
FREE DAILY TRAINING:

ABOUT THIS POCKET GUIDE

This is your "Pocket Guide" for how to sell. A pocket guide is a small book you can read in under 30 minutes, solves the exact problem you have, and fits nicely in your pocket so you can always reference it.

To grow a multi-million dollar company, you need to learn three things:

1. How to sell.
2. How to hire and train people to sell for you.
3. How to manage those people to keep selling at scale.

This pocket guide is the first of a three-part series.

The 12-Phase Sales Script I am revealing to you in this guide is called the **Big Money Script**. I call it that because whenever anyone uses it, they make big money.

Use this **Big Money Script** when selling prospects on the phone. It's the exact script I've used to sell $30M of my own advice, online courses, coaching, and high-ticket seminars. The only way to get it was to become part of a $10,000 coaching program.

Why on earth would I give this script away for a measly few bucks when I used to charge $10,000 for access to it?

Well, the first reason is that I retired as a coach. Now I release free training on YouTube that I used to charge thousands of dollars for. And the reason I do that? I want to help you build your company to the point where you need a sales team. That way, you can hire CloseDeals.com to either build one for you—or take over management of your existing team and BLOW UP your sales.

That is what we sell, and I am willing to give you upfront value and training for FREE to get you to a place where you can take advantage of our service. And if that is something you don't need, helping you make more money is fine with me.

If you don't own a company, you can still use this script to sell someone else's product and make big commissions. You can even apply to become a Certified Closer for CloseDeals.com. We will not only help you master this script but we can also place you with a company where you can make $10,000 per month or MORE in commissions as a remote salesperson. Some of our closers even earn over $25,000 per month.

If you're a business owner or a sales rep and you'd like to inquire about our products and services, email hello@closedeals.com.

If you're looking for help overcoming objections when dealing with tough prospects, marketing techniques, and other ways to grow your business, you can get additional pocket guides here: CloseDeals.com/books.

WHO THIS BOOK IS FOR

This book is specifically designed for salespeople who want to earn more commissions or business owners who want to sell more of their high-ticket products and services such as ...

- Coaching or Consulting
- Online Courses
- Masterminds
- Professional Services
- Agency Services
- Events and Seminar
- High-End Software
- Done-for-you Services

Bottom line, if you are selling your own high-end products and services, this book will help you sell more—as well as train your salespeople to do so.

If you are a salesperson who wants to create more commissions, this book will help you do exactly that. And if you ever decide to start your own business, this book will teach you the skill that will not only serve you today as a commissioned salesperson but also in the future as an entrepreneur.

This skill will enrich every part of your life.

HOW I LEARNED TO SELL

Before I became an 8-figure earner, a *WSJ* bestselling author, and a real estate investor, I was delivering pizzas as a college dropout.

I grew up in a small Florida town as an only child. My home was not a happy one. I'll often recall holidays and birthdays where they would scream and throw things at each other. On multiple occasions, the police were even called. I love my mother and father, and they're great when they're apart, but they were not so great together.

Since I had no siblings, it was challenging for me to integrate into the school system. I didn't know how to interact with other children, and as a result, I got bullied incessantly. With very few friends, I didn't get invited to many parties. That means I had a lot of time to read.

I became obsessed with reading and learned many skills I knew I could show others and help them. But no one ever took me seriously, let alone actually listened to me. And so, I never got to share these amazing things I learned.

Have you ever felt you had something amazing to share that could help people, but no one would listen to you? It's a horrible feeling.

This is why when I go to conferences and people recognize me, I always take time to talk to them and take a picture. Because I know what it feels like to be ignored, and I don't want to make anyone feel that way.

Eventually, my father considered pulling me out of school. In my first close ever, I convinced him to let me enroll in a homeschooling program where I could complete high school through a self-education program. My grades were so good that I qualified for a program where my parents didn't even have to tutor me. I could read the materials myself and then take the tests. While this solved the problem of getting bullied at school, it perpetuated my problem of having limited social skills.

To be a great salesperson, wouldn't you agree that the number one thing you need to have is social skills? I think you would. But I didn't have that, yet here I am today, one of the highest-selling online entrepreneurs in the world.

This is because I learned a skill that not only helped me make millions selling my own product, but that product was the very thing people never wanted from me my entire life—my advice.

I sold $30 million worth of my own consulting, coaching, and seminars, and the skill that made that possible … was the skill of selling.

The journey to learning that skill began one fateful day when I responded to a Craigslist ad. The ad offered $50,000 per year or more to be a traveling salesperson, selling at stores like Costco and Sam's Club. They made it clear that they required at least five years of sales experience.

Before this, I had been delivering pizza for seven years straight. Although most people deliver pizza for a couple of years, I was on my way to delivering for a decade. I was over it. I needed something new. I needed a way to break free.

So even though I did not have five years of sales experience, I applied anyway and said I had the experience. It was one of the few times I had been dishonest in my life, but my desperation clouded my judgment.

By some miracle, I passed the phone interview, and they flew me up to New Jersey for two weeks of training. When I got there, I discovered that this company was training people to become "Pitch Men." Yes, kind of like Billy Mays, the OxiClean guy. In fact, I was told that this was where Billy Mays got his start. And my sales manager was actually his sales manager early in his career.

My sales manager pulled me aside a few days into the training and called me out. He said, "You don't have any sales experience, do you?"

I broke down and admitted that I didn't. I told him why I applied and even the story of my upbringing. I sounded like a gushing idiot.

"Well, we already paid for you to come up here, and honestly, I admire your boldness. So I'll make you a deal. If you can read this script word for word, I promise you that not only will people listen to you, they will buy from you. If you can do that, I'll forget that you don't have sales experience."

I agreed and worked my ass off to do exactly what he said.

We went to Sam's Club for a trial run a week later. I was selling Titanium Cookware, just one alternative to your garden-variety Teflon pans. He showed me how to set up the booth, display all the pots and pans so they looked pretty, and prepare for my first show.

He walked up to the loudspeaker microphone and said the following ...

"Attention Sam's Club shoppers. In five minutes, we will be doing a cooking show on aisle 14. We will give you a free gift if you attend the show and stay till the end. So please make your way there now."

Over the next five minutes, about 20 people gathered in front of my booth. Finally, it was my time to "read the words." My stomach was in knots, and in an instant, I regretted answering that ad more than any decision I'd ever made.

I began sweating, and my leg wouldn't stop shaking. My sales manager gave me a look and silently mouthed, "Just say the words." So I turned on my brain, opened my mouth, and said the exact words I was trained to say.

Over the next 20 minutes, I saw people raise their eyebrows and pay attention to me for the first time in my life. They hung on every word I said. And 20 minutes later, five people gave me $500 for a cookware set — $500 for a set of cookware when every other set in that store was a fraction of that price.

My commission was $250. I made $250 in 20 minutes. Then I did it again 4 more times that day for a grand total of $1,000 in my pocket, just by saying the words.

It worked. I said the words I was told to say, and not only did everyone listen to me, but they also gave me money. And they gave me a lot more money for essentially the same product they could have bought for a much lower price.

That was when I realized that if I knew what to say and how to say it, I could make the world bend to my will. Ok, maybe that sounds a little villainous, but I could at least make a lot of money!

I spent the next 10 years learning everything I could about sales and marketing. I became obsessed with it. The more I learned, the more I earned. The more I earned, the more I invested in learning more.

I routinely spent tens of thousands of dollars on courses and masterminds, and I've multiple times spent $50,000 for a one-on-one day with masters of the craft. The truth is, that's why I became so effective at selling. That's why I had million-dollar months and even a couple of million-dollar days selling from stage.

I once sold 34 spots into a $30,000 mastermind with only 158 people on a Zoom. This was at the very beginning of the pandemic when no one was allowed to leave their home. I had one camera, a whiteboard, and a Zoom link. That's it.

That's how powerful learning to sell can be! My grandfather always said, *"No matter the state of the economy, if you can sell, you will never be broke."*

I took that skill of selling, a skill that made all my dreams come true, and decided to teach it to others. This made me $30M in courses, consulting, and seminars. I've since retired from consulting to focus on CloseDeals.com where we build and manage your sales team so you don't have to.

Why do I help others with selling? Because somewhere, there is a little boy or a girl who is afraid to talk to other children, scared to join in, afraid to speak up—because when they do, they are harassed and silenced. They are bullied into suppressing their dreams.

They were not born with a silver tongue, and those children grow up to be suppressed adults, never realizing their true potential. Most of the time, those suppressed souls have something amazing to share with the world, but they don't know what to say to make people listen, let alone make people buy.

And I know beyond a shadow of a doubt that I can teach them the words to say to make anything possible in their life. Why? Because I've done it over a thousand times, literally. Through our free and paid content, I've helped create thousands of 6-figure companies, hundreds of 7-figure companies, and over a dozen 8-figure companies by teaching them these words.

In this book, I reveal one part of those words—a simple sales script you can use to sell your products and services and sell them for a higher price than your competitors. Just like those pots and pans so many years ago.

Keep this pocket guide on your desk, in your pocket, and more importantly, give it to your salespeople. (You can buy these in bulk at CloseDeals.com/books.)

We have other guides on hiring and training salespeople, managing salespeople, overcoming objections, and more. However, this guide specifically focuses on what to say on a sales call. I hope it serves you, and if it does, please share it with others!

THE BIG MONEY SCRIPT

The Big Money Script breaks down the 12 phases of a sale:

I. Rapport

II. Expectations

III. Decision Makers

IV. The Reason

V. Dig

VI. Tried

VII. Current and Desired Situation

VIII. Why

IX. Admission

X. Commitment

XI. Customized Close

XII. Price

WARNING: DO NOT FOLLOW THIS SCRIPT

The purpose of the 12 phases of a sale is to gather information from the prospect so you can make a customized pitch at the end of the call—one that makes perfect sense to them. If you ask questions in a certain phase, and the customers give you the answers to the degree you need, then simply skip over the questions in the next phase or skip that phase altogether. Do not treat this as a "script" but rather a framework to get the data you need to make the sale. If you already have the data, move on!

#1 GOLDEN RULE

If a prospect is ready to buy, let them buy. Do not make the mistake of forcing the prospect to go through this entire script if they are already ready to buy.

If at some point during the call this prospect makes it clear that they are already aware of the price and want it, just sell it to them.

PRO TIP

When someone answers your questions, say as little as possible. Do not engage in chit-chat (other than in the rapport section), go off on a tangent, tell a story (unless handling an objection) or expand on ANYTHING. They should do 95% of the talking. In other words, SAY AS LITTLE AS POSSIBLE.

PHASE 1: RAPPORT

This is the first few minutes of the call. This is where you engage in some chit-chat to develop **Rapport**. Ask where they're from. Ask how their week is going. Find something you can connect with.

One great way to make this easy is to look them up on social media and find something they are interested in that you know about, so you can talk about common interests.

I like to start off by saying, ***"Where are you calling in from? Oh [CITY NAME]?"***

- I remember visiting there …
- My Dad is actually from there …
- Oh, isn't it pretty warm/cold there this time of year …

People love buying from people they can relate to, and *the easiest way to relate is to find common ground.* The easiest way to find common ground is to *get people to talk about themselves.*

People love talking about themselves. The more you get them to talk about themselves, the more you learn about them, the more rapport you will build. To get them talking about themselves, use the following tactics …

Mirroring: To get your prospects to talk about themselves, mirror them. If you want them to expand on something, repeat the last few words of what they said with an upward inflection in your voice. For example:

- **Prospect:** *Yeah, we moved here two years ago to raise our children.*
- **You:** *Oh really? To raise your children?*
- **Prospect:** *Yeah, we didn't like the school system in Chicago.*
- **You:** *You didn't like the school system in Chicago?*
- **Prospect:** *Yeah, it's too liberal. We don't want our children to become indoctrinated.* [BAM! There it is! We just found out something about them, now we use it.]
- **You:** *Yeah, I get that, no way I'm putting my kid through that either. I'd rather homeschool.*
- **Prospect:** *Totally! It's crazy what they are doing now!* [BAM! Common ground achieved!]

Matching: To be even more relatable, match their energy. If they are reserved, be reserved. If they are high energy, be high energy. People buy from people they can relate to. The most fundamental way to relate is to exist on the same energy vibration.

PHASE 2: EXPECTATIONS

This phase is where you set **Expectations**. You lay out the format of the call and get them to AGREE to that format. When you get a prospect to agree to a format of a conversation, it's much easier to ask the prospect to return to the agreed-upon format to keep control of the conversation.

My favorite way to do this goes as follows …

You: *Are you ready to get started [FIRST NAME]?*

Them: *Sure.*

You: *So this is how these calls usually go …* [You are framing this in a way that gets them to simply accept how things are, rather than telling them what to do.]

It's kind of like going to the doctor, I'm going to ask you a few questions about your business [or health, investments, mindset, etc.] *and what you're struggling with, figure out what the problem is, give you a diagnosis, just like a doctor would, and then suggest a solution, kind of like a doctor would suggest a treatment or prescription.*

If the solution is something we can provide, and we believe we can solve your problem, then I'll tell you more about what we have to offer and let you decide if you want to become a part of it or not.

Sound good?

Them: *Sure, sounds good.*

You have now taken full control of the sales call by not only telling them exactly how the call will go but also getting them to agree to the format. When you get a prospect to agree to a format of a conversation, it's much easier to keep that conversation on track.

If you don't frame the conversation this way, there is no clarity in how the conversation will go, and then the conversation will turn into chaos. There is no sale in chaos. There is only a sale in clarity.

Once they have agreed to the format, you can now move on to the next phase.

PHASE 3: DECISION MAKERS

The purpose of this phase is to identify who needs to be on the call for a decision to be made. If at all possible, you want to get all **Decision Makers** on the call. If you only get one, they will attempt to relay the information to their partner at a separate time and they will NOT do a good job, trust me. They also won't be able to answer questions or overcome objections. So while it is not ALWAYS possible to get both partners on the call, it's highly recommended.

My partner and COO of CloseDeals.com, Phil Bohol, helped me out with the section because I absolutely LOVE his take on how to address this, more than the way I have traditionally done it, which is using my gut.

GET ALL DECISIONS MAKERS ON THE CALL — FROM PHIL BOHOL

Most salespeople ask the following question when trying to make sure the decision maker is on the call:

"Do you need to get your spouse on the call to make a decision?"

But what I've found works the best is integrating it so that it's so conversational that it doesn't even sound like you're asking the question.

There are two ways to discover the decision maker, and the second one is more advanced as you reach unconscious competence (the gut feeling). That's what Dan does, and he goes by feel on whether or not they need to be on the call to make the sale.

But if you're still working on your closing skill, I would recommend practicing #1, which is what I'll explain to you now.

As you build trust and rapport, you'll want to ask them about themselves like you're catching up with an old friend you haven't seen for a few years (think of it as getting an update on their life).

When they tell you what they're doing for work, you transition to get to the spouse or business partner topic in a way that sounds like a regular conversation …

I totally forgot to ask you, are you on your own right now, or are you taking care of a family?

If they say they are on their own, it's safe to move forward since they have no family or spouse that they mentioned.

If they say they have a family they take care of, depending on the rapport, you can simply follow up with …

What does your spouse do for a living?

They will respond, and you acknowledge then ask, *"Are they supportive of you wanting to possibly get [END RESULT]?"*

You want to know if their spouse is supportive of them wanting to get help with losing weight, making more money, leaving their 9-to-5 to work from home, etc.

If they say yes, which usually they do, move on to asking about their kids. This way it feels like you're casually getting to know them and it alleviates any sales pressure.

If you're on a B2B offer or closing business owners, the question sequence is the same. Instead of asking about their life partner, you can ask, *"I totally forgot to ask, do you run the business on your own right now or do you have a business partner helping you out?"*

If they say they are on their own, you can move forward. If they say, "I have a business partner helping out," you can directly ask …

When it comes to making decisions with potentially working with an outside company to help you, what is your decision-making process with your business partner before possibly moving forward?

Now you know if they need their partner or not, and if they do, you can ask if they are available to come on the call or reschedule when they are both present.

THE SILENT KILLER TIP — FROM DAN

If both partners are on the call, you can often identify which one is **The Silent Killer**. The talker is the one that does the most talking and interacts with you the most frequently. Many times this is the husband and the wife stays somewhat quiet, or vice versa. If it's a business partner, there will usually be one that is more forward and one that is more silent.

The one that is more silent is the one you must watch out for. We call this **The Silent Killer.** They're the ones who will keep quiet until it's time to deny the sale. You want to make sure they feel heard and respected. Get them to chime in, and get them to ask questions or offer objections so that you can overcome them.

You do not want to wait until the end of the call when they spent the last hour hearing you give all the attention to their partner. Now you make the pitch, and you basically have to start all over with them. Not good.

PHASE 4: THE REASON

In this section of the sales call, you want to get the prospect to verbally state **The Reason** for the call. Even if you think that's obvious, they need to SAY it so it's front of mind. We need to get them thinking about

WHY they are on this call in the first place and the pain that surrounds that reason. People buy when they feel the cost of feeling the pain is far more than the cost of removing it. We need them to FEEL the pain by talking about that pain out loud.

Start by asking them why they booked a call today and what they need your help with specifically.

My favorite way to do this is by saying the following …

You: *So the first thing I always like to ask is, why did you book a call to speak to me today? What do you need my help with specifically?*

There are really two questions here, and sometimes people will answer both in their response. But it's important to follow up if they don't.

Them: *Well, I saw that you [did notable thing] and thought that was impressive. I really need help with [problem] because [reason it's so important now].*

This is the perfect answer, but rarely will you get it in this format. They will usually tell you one of the two points, for instance …

Them: *Well, I really need help with [problem].*

This is good because we got them to say exactly what they need help with. They said it out loud so it's front of mind, which is what we want. What we *don't* want is for their problem to be "out of sight, out of mind." But they did not mention *why* they reached out to us specifically out of every possible option. So you say …

You: *Got it. So you reached out because you need help with [problem], but why did you reach out to us of all people?*

You want to do this so that they validate your authority and credibility. You don't want to tell them you are credible, you want THEM to say you're credible.

Them: *Well, I saw that you [did notable thing] and thought I could really use your help.*

Now, this is exactly what you want to hear, but if they mention that they don't know much about your company, that at least tells you that they are unaware of your credibility and authority. You can mention some of your accolades as a direct response to, "I don't know much about your company." Mentioning accolades without being asked sounds desperate, but in this case, you are *engineering the ask.*

However, if they already know of your credibility and authority, then you say …

You: *Got it. So you reached out to me because you saw we have a great reputation in the space, and you specifically want help with [problem].*

NOW you say the most important thing of all …

You: *But why now? Why is it so important to solve this right now?*

Them: *Well, we just had [event] happen and it's really stressing us out.*

So now you have THE most important piece of the puzzle—the pain. You will likely only get a preview of this pain. In Phase 5, we will stir that pain.

To give you a real-life example, let's say someone is reaching out to us to inquire about working with CloseDeals.com to manage their sales team.

Us: *So the first thing I always like to ask is, why did you book a call to speak to me today? What do you need my help with specifically?*

Them: *Well, I saw that one of your founders, Dan Henry, did $30 million in high ticket sales with a sales team, and I really need help selling more of our products without me doing all the sales calls.*

Us: *Got it! So you reached out to me because you saw we have a great reputation in the space, and you specifically want my help with growing your business, but why now? Why is it so important right now?*

Them: *Well, we just had a baby and I know that I can't be taking sales calls all day, but I also really don't know how to hire or manage a sales team. So it's really* *important that we still make sales but I have time to spend with my new son.*

BAM. Now we have the REAL pain, and it's not making more sales. It's spending time with their newborn baby. It's family. So at this point we realize we are not helping them make more sales, we are helping them build a family THROUGH sales, and THAT is what the call becomes about.

PHASE 5: DIG

This phase can be skipped if they really went DEEP on why they need help in Phase 4, but most of the time you need to **Dig** into the pain. They need to FEEL how horrible it is to continue to have their problem not solved.

So we need to get a specific answer and in detail. If you get a general answer, simply say, "Can you expand on that? Tell me more about that."

Some additional ways to bring out the pain are ...

- *Why do you think this problem exists?*
- *What have you tried to fix it?*
- *How long has this been a problem?*
- *Is this problem affecting your life in other ways, and how?*

In the case of the person who told us they don't want to take their own sales calls or manage their sales team, the real reason was that they want to spend more time with their newborn.

Us: *Oh, boy or girl? What's his name? Charlie? Ah, cute. You know, a lot of parents hire nannies and night nurses, but it sounds like you really value the connection with your child. What makes that so important to you?*

Them: *Well, my father never spent much time with me as a kid, so I don't want to do that to my kid.*

Us: *Your father never spent a lot of time with you?* **[Mirroring]**

Them: *Yeah, I mean, honestly it affected me and my sister in a lot of ways.*

Us: *Oh really? How so?* [Make sure to squeeze your eyebrows together to convey concern when asking something sensitive.]

Them: *Well, we never had a male role model, or anyone to teach us how to ride a bike, or for me how to learn how to fix things around the house. My mother always hired handymen.*

Us: *So it sounds like you really don't want your son Charlie to have that same experience?*

PRO RAPPORT TIP

Use "sounds like" whenever a prospect tells you something and you want to connect with them, show them you are listening, and validate their experience at the same time. It will also get them to keep talking without resistance.

Them: *Yeah, no way, I swore I would never let that happen to him, that's why I want to be there for him.*

Us: *Got it. Well, I really hope we can help you make that happen. Mind if I ask you a few more questions to make sure we can make that a reality?*

You see, we are NOT selling sales management. We are selling what sales management GETS him! The thing that he has thought about his entire life. Undoing the wrong his Dad did to him and never letting his child go through that.

We started at *"I need help with sales"* and ended with a riveting and intimate story about his father. When the prospect is thinking about THAT (instead of your offer) that's when it's 100X easier to get them to BUY your offer.

Bottom line, if they don't get a little upset, you are not doing your job. Being able to do this in a way that makes the customer upset, while simultaneously making them feel like you care, is a SKILL. It's a skill that needs to be taught, developed, and nurtured.

I'd love to tell you this part is easy, but I'd be lying. If you are selling your own offer, it's going to be hard because there is no one to push you.

We spend 7 weeks drilling our closers, or at least 4 weeks drilling closers that we come on to manage.

Even after all that, it still takes daily nurturing for the entirety of their tenure as a salesperson. But the reward is worth it. My sales team made my company $30 million, and I rarely had to take a sales call. In my opinion, it's worth the time it takes to help your team develop this skill.

PRO TIP

Try to never ask, *"Why?"* when a prospect tells you how they feel or what they believe. Don't say, *"Why did it affect you?"* It's jarring. You could elicit a negative response. This is because as children, when we do something wrong, most parents say, *"Why did you do that?"* This programs us to dislike when someone asks, *"why"* we think or behave a certain way.

It's much better to say WHAT or HOW:

- *What makes you say that?*
- *How did you come to that conclusion?*
- *What do you think is the reason for that?*
- *How do you think that happened?*

PHASE 6: TRIED

Midway through the call, we need to know what they have **Tried** so far. At this point, they should be at an emotional peak. So the next question should make them gush information a lot more than if you asked this randomly.

What have you tried so far to fix this?

Not only does this further bring out the pain of their frustration of trying to solve this all on their own, but we also need to know what they have already tried in case we need to explain how our product is different. Most of the time, we either offer something different than the things that they have already tried, or we offer them in a way that is more effective.

We need to know this, so we don't say something later in the call that elicits the response, *"I've already tried that, it doesn't work."* This is a sales **DEATH SENTENCE** because now they start getting the idea in their head that either you aren't listening or you don't know how to help. Even if they didn't make you aware of it.

If you know what they have already tried, then you either don't say that thing, or you say it a different way. For instance, if you are selling a coaching program that teaches speakers how to book more gigs, and they say they have tried cold calling event organizers …

Instead of saying, *"We show you how to cold call event organizers …"*

Knowing they have already tried this, you could say, *"We give you our proven cold script, a script 99% of speakers don't use, because they don't know it exists. I know you have tried cold calls before, but so has everyone else in our program. Once they use this script, they are shocked as to how quickly they book gigs."*

This diffuses their objection before they can even make it. But you would not know this unless you find out what they have already tried.

PHASE 7: CURRENT AND DESIRED SITUATION

Now we need to know where they are and where they want to be. The first question in Phase 7 revolves around identifying where exactly they are in the journey to solving that problem and what that looks like. This is their **Current Situation**.

Unless you have already learned this, ask exactly where they are using the most quantifiable metrics in their situation. If they are trying to make money, ask how much money they are currently making. If they are trying to lose weight, ask them what their current weight is. If they are trying to speak on stage, ask them how many gigs they are booking per month.

For instance, if you are selling weight loss, this question is as simple as, *"I'd like to know where we are so I can better understand where we are going. Are you opposed to sharing your current weight?"*

PRO TIP

To soften the ask for sensitive information, frame it as *"Are you opposed to."* Human beings are conditioned to say NO to salespeople more than YES. It's much easier for them to say, *"No, I am not opposed,"* rather than, *"Yes, I'm OK with sharing."* This is a small touch, but over the course of hundreds of sales calls, it can make a major impact in your sales. Also, by this point in the conversation, you should have built enough rapport with them to make them feel comfortable with sharing.

Depending on what they have shared so far about why they are on the call and what they have already tried, my team at CloseDeals.com might ask:

- *What is your team's current close rate?*
- *How many hours a week are you spending taking your own sales calls?*
- *How many leads do you have and what percentage of those leads are you turning into sales?*

Next, we find out where they want to be. This is their **Desired Situation.**

There is an old saying, *"Expectation is the root of all heartache."* It's also the root of a bad sales call! So we need to set proper expectations ALWAYS.

We must find out what they want or what would make them happy, then make sure we can not only deliver but also articulate that we can deliver, and they will be happy.

You could ask, *"If you were to work with us or enroll in our program, where would you want to be 12 months from now to feel like the investment was more than worth it?"*

PRO TIP

> The reason we don't simply ask where they want to be, and instead ask where they would like to be *to make the investment worth it*, is to make sure the customer sets the lowest possible expectations so that we can over-deliver.

If we simply ask where they want to be, they'll probably say something like: *A million dollars! I wanna be a super-model! I want my dog to be featured in the Westminster dog show!*

Now whatever we promise or offer may seem like a letdown if they shoot too high. But if we simply ask what will make the investment worth it, customers will likely give a much more reasonable response, and oftentimes one that you can easily exceed.

Another thing to be careful of is talking about your best results or making a specific claim. At least right away …

If you say that you could help them lose 50 pounds, or that most of your clients lose 50 pounds, and they end up losing 40 pounds after buying your product, they will still feel a bit let down even though they lost a ton of weight!

But if they tell you it would be worth it if they lost 15 pounds, and they end up losing 30 pounds, now you have more than exceeded their expectations and they will sing your praises from the mountaintops.

And when prospects see existing customers sing your praises, it makes everything I'm teaching you in this guide that much more effective.

Now, if you find they still come out with an unrealistic expectation, you can bring them back down to earth by using the **Down to Earth Close.**

For instance, if someone was speaking to my team about helping them with sales, we might say:

Well, I understand you want to make an extra $5 million this year in your business, and I think that is a fantastic goal. But just to make sure that we set realistic expectations, if we were to increase your sales rate by just 25% and completely take the weight of managing your sales team off your shoulders, based on your numbers, that would be an extra $1 million in sales for you this year. If all we helped you make was an extra million dollars this year in your business, would you be more than happy?

They will, of course, say yes, and now you have used the **Down to Earth Close** to reset expectations.

THE DOWN TO EARTH CLOSE SCRIPT

Well, I understand you want [unrealistic expectation], and I think that is a fantastic goal. But just to make sure that we set realistic expectations, if we were to achieve [realistic expectation and what it would mean to them] … if all we helped you achieve was [realistic expectation], would you be more than happy?

Once you know where they are and where they want to be, you can move on to the most important question of all. Their WHY.

PHASE 8: WHY

This is the phase where we understand **WHY** they want the **Desired Situation**. Why do they want the result that they want? Do they just want to make more money? What are they going to do with it? Buy a house? Why? Because the wife wants a bigger home and she has been asking for years? You'll find in many cases like this that they don't really want more money, they just don't want their wife to leave them. Or they don't want to be a disappointment to their kids.

We are going to rehash **Phase 4** and dig deeper into the reasons why they want the problem solved. We are earning the right to do this and bring it back up by associating it with a specific result. This way it does not seem redundant.

So we might say something like …

- *OK great, so you'll be happy if you lost 50 pounds?*
- *OK great, you'd be happy if you made an extra million dollars?*
- *OK great, you'd be happy if your dog was a 7 out of 10 on the obedience scale?*

Now ask them why they want the result they want. But don't ask, "Why?" Instead, ask, *"What is driving you to want XYZ"* or *"How would your life be different if you had XYZ?"*

Remember to use WHAT or HOW in lieu of WHY whenever possible.

- *May I ask what is driving you to achieve that goal? In other words, if you made an extra million dollars, how would that affect you or change your life? What would that look like?*
- *May I ask what is driving you to lose 50 pounds? In other words, if you lost 50 pounds how would that change your life? What would that look like?*

PRO TIP

The best way to get someone to freely share specifics about why they want what they want, is to simply ask, *"What would that look like?"* This is a non-aggressive way to get the info you need without seeming nosy.

At this point, they're going to begin sharing the reason why, and you can use mirroring and the "sounds like" closes to dig deeper and have them bring those reasons out into the open like you did in Phase 5.

Now if you get some resistance here, a great thing I learned to say to completely shut that down is the following ...

The reason why I'm asking what your life would look like if you had an extra million dollars is that our founder absolutely loves to feature customer success stories. He's obsessed with sharing his customers' wins. But the thing is, no one likes to hear that someone made money and that's it. They love to hear what changed in their life as a result of the money. It's much more powerful if we share that you had more children and so your wife wanted a bigger house, and you were able to give that to her. Or if your mother was dying of cancer and you needed the money to pay for her treatment.

Then I used to make them laugh by saying, *"Unless all you want is a Lamborghini."* This always got a chuckle and completely shut down their resistance, while also showing them a genuine reason why we are asking these questions.

On a Personal Note: I am that founder who is obsessed with sharing customer success stories. What I've discovered is that no one gives a shit that you made $1 million. They give a shit about what changed in your life as a result—because they want to see their life change as well.

The truth is, whether you buy anything from me or not, it won't change anything about my life. I will still wake up in the same house, drive the same car, eat the same food, and go on the same vacations. But it could change *your* life. And when it does, and I get to hear about it, I get to relive that moment in some small way, over and over again. There's nothing like it.

FUN FACT

The reason **WHY** you want something always comes down to either **LOVE** or **STATUS**. If you want to lose weight, it's either because you want to look good (status) or you want to live longer (love for yourself) or you want to be around longer for your children (love).

If you want to make more money, it could be because you want to finally be seen as a success (status) or you don't want your wife to leave (love) or you want to send your kids to college (love).

Status: When I started investing in real estate, I would go look at investment properties, but I would never get a callback. I basically looked like a kid because I was in my twenties. No one would take me seriously. But after I bought a Rolex watch, I started getting callbacks. That purchase worked like a charm to elevate my status.

Love: I remember when my mom quit her high-paying corporate sales job because she was distraught over her divorce from my stepdad. It completely derailed her life. She ended up going from the nice suburban home I grew up in to living in a trailer park and barely being able to pay her bills. The moment I bought her a brand new house, even nicer than the one I grew up in, the look on her face meant everything to me. For the rest of my life, I will never forget that moment.

Every buying decision comes down to love or status. We must find out which one we're dealing with and what that looks like for our customers.

PHASE 9: ADMISSION

Now comes the most important phase of the call, the **Admission**. We need to get them to ADMIT that they need help.

IMPORTANT: You must absolutely get them to admit, essentially, that they don't know what the heck they are doing or they desperately need help. If they don't think they need help, you cannot sell them. And even if they said they need help, if they don't say it out loud, you cannot sell them.

You simply ask, *"What is stopping you from achieving this all on your own without any help?"*

This one I learned from Sam Ovens who I consider an amazing marketer and a dear friend.

You're looking for one of three answers, and if you've done everything correctly up to this point, your prospect should say something like:

- I don't know how to do it.
- I want to follow a proven process from someone that's already done it.
- I want to get there faster.

Do not make the mistake of moving on from this phase without getting a reply that's similar to at least one of these top three responses.

PHASE 10: COMMITMENT

Once they have **Admitted** they need help, we must secure **Commitment** from the customer that they need and want to solve this problem right away.

A good way I've found to do this is to simply ask, *"When are you wanting to fix this?"*

If they say NOW, you say, *"I understand that you want to fix it now, but how committed are you to making that happen? Will you do the work? Will you take action? Are you coachable? Will you get us the information we need to get started?"*

Ask whatever makes sense for your offer to make sure they are willing to do their part. You make it less about the sale, *and all about them doing their part.* Once they say YES and offer commitment, you can move on to the next phase.

If, however, they say they want to get started in a month or something like that, here are some questions you can ask to get them to realize they need to offer commitment now:

- *What makes you say a month?*
- *Any reason you don't want to fix it right now?*
- *You booked a call for today, so what is making you want to wait?*

Many times you will receive a response like, *"You're right, I really do need to fix this now."*

If you don't, you can use the **Procrastination Close:**

Would you say it's accurate that up until this call, you have been putting off solving this problem? How many times have you said that next month or now is not a good time? And how has that worked out for you?

The truth is, we are not defined by how we react in times of triumph but by how we react in times of struggle. Anyone can win when conditions are perfect, but a true champion wins when the conditions are not ideal.

The fact is, it's never a good time. It's never a good time to call your mother, it's never a good time to start a new weight-loss program, and it's never a good time to fix a major problem in your business. And even if you think a later time is a good time, you know something will come up. Life will keep happening. If you truly want to solve this problem, would you agree that you have to commit to solving it even when it's not the perfect time?

Another great way to secure commitment is to play into the "we want what we can't have" part of the human psyche. This is especially effective when the prospect is being difficult or stubborn.

In this case, you can do a **Take Away Close** like our closers do at CloseDeals.com:

"Dan only works with people that are ready to go. You don't have to work with Dan, I'm not here to convince you. I'm just here to see if you're a good fit."

or …

"Listen, we don't do high-pressure sales, in fact, the opposite. If you are not committed to [getting result] or you don't want to join/invest in our product, then we can end the call right now. No sweat. But if you are wanting to solve this problem, let's talk about how we can make that happen. Which would you like to do?"

Believe it or not, this works FAR more times than it doesn't. Plus let's be honest, you really don't want to sell something to someone who is going to limp in. If they come in with a poor attitude, they won't get results or they will be a difficult client, and then it makes your whole brand look bad. ***Correct the attitude before collecting the money.***

Once you secure commitment, you can move on to Phase 11.

SIDENOTE: When you get resistance like this from a prospect, these are called objections. Handling objections is the other side of the coin to a sales script. If the call goes swimmingly, the sales script will convert the prospect into a sale without any objections.

Unless you are a Jedi salesperson, you will get objections. Handling those objections is a skill all in itself. I have written a dedicated guide to handling objections which you can find at CloseDeals.com/books. I highly suggest you pick that one up and leave it on your desk where you take your sales calls.

PHASE 11: CUSTOMIZED CLOSE

This is the bread and butter of the entire script. If you've done everything correctly up to this point, you're about to deliver a pitch to the customer that will literally feel like the entire offer, product, or service was specifically made for them.

You'll want to describe the customer identity as how they described themselves. Describe the thing they want as how they described it. And describe whatever the most relevant portion of your program or product is that can get them what they want.

It will feel like the day they were born, the doctor pulled them out of the womb and said, *"We're gonna make a product specifically for this little baby right here."*

So now you say something like, *"OK, I believe I have enough information now and honestly, I believe we can help you. Would you like me to share how?*

PRO TIP

Never say *"I think."* Always say, *"I believe." "Think"* makes it sound like you aren't sure. *"Believe"* sounds like you are sure. People love believers.

✗ *I think we can help you. Would you like me to share how?*

☑ *I believe we can help you. Would you like me to share how?*

They will most undoubtedly say YES, and then you use the following **Customized Close** framework to make your pitch …

Well, our area of expertise is helping [CUSTOMER IDENTITY] to get [RESULT THEY WANT] so they can get [BYPRODUCT OF RESULT]. And we do that by [OFFER]. Now, this may not be for you, but I'll let you decide. Does that sound like a good fit so far?

PRO TIP

When you say, "This may not be for you," it puts the customer in a frame of mind where they want to justify why it is for them. Humans always want what they can't have. So it makes them commit even more to your offer—especially after the offer you have explained is obviously perfect for them.

This customer will almost always say yes because it *has* to be a fit. All we did was literally repeat back to them exactly who they are, what their problem is, and what they will get as a result of solving the problem.

Using an example from CloseDeals.com, let's say that one of our closers was on a sales call with a solopreneur. She says she's making $50,000 per month and taking her own sales calls, but she wants to break 6-figures per month so she can spend more time with her newborn baby. Someone from my team would say something like …

Our area of expertise is helping solopreneurs, who do their own sales calls, break into 6-figure months so they can spend more time with their family and not be on the phone all day. And we do that by placing one of our certified closers with your company, training them on your offer, and managing them each and every day to consistently close your sales calls so you don't have to. Does that sound like a good fit so far?

But if, instead, she says she has a sales team of three people but she's pulling her hair out trying to get them to consistently close, she's always hiring and firing salespeople, and now she's pausing ads because her people can't close, then we might say …

Our area of expertise is helping high ticket entrepreneurs who have a small sales team of 3-5 people, increase the close rate, keep them closing the leads they have so you can keep marketing, and manage them each and every day so that you don't have to. This means we review their call recordings, make sure they fill out their end-of-day reports, and motivate them to push harder to hit sales records. Does that sound like a fit so far?

Either way, she should say YES.

Now even though those sound like two different offers, they are essentially the same. And we at CloseDeals.com offer both. The difference is very slight, but the way in which your offer is articulated can be worlds apart.

It's your articulation that will make the sale, not your offer. The only way to properly articulate it is to ask questions and plug the answers into that articulation.

Once they confirm that it's a fit, you immediately ask, *"Great! Can I share how it works?"*

At this point, you are going to **assume the sale** and walk them through what it will be like when they sign on with your company. You're not going to ask them for money, or if they have their credit card ready, or any of that old-school nonsense. You are going to assume they have already bought, and you are doing nothing more than walking them through the onboarding process.

This is called the **How It Works Pitch**. You will need to develop your own **How It Works Pitch** as that's not something I can show you how to create in a little booklet, but I can give you an example. All you really have to do is know what happens from the time they sign up to the time they begin getting results and explain that process step-by-step while framing it as a benefit to them. This will be unique and custom to your product and business.

THIS IS THE CLOSEDEALS.COM "HOW IT WORKS" PITCH:

So your next call will be with your Account Executive Karla. She's going to do an onboarding interview where she asks a set of very specific questions that will let us know everything we need to learn about your offer.

These are questions Dan developed over the past several years in his sales and marketing consulting practice to immediately understand everything he needs to know about a client's business. We now take those questions and use them to develop a debriefing for your new closer, or if you already have a sales team, to bring your closers fully up to speed on what they need to change to sell more of your offer.

We will then assign your company a sales manager from our team, and they will begin training your salespeople to sell the dickens out of your offer. This process takes 10 to 14 days.

Once that is complete, we begin the management process where we do daily huddles to motivate them to crush sales for the day. We make sure they fill out their end-of-day reports. We run objection-handling drills to make sure their skills stay sharp, and we work with them on about 20 other proven sales levers that they can pull to instantly increase your revenue. Not to mention we show them how to reactivate old leads and make instant sales you didn't even know were there. Most of our clients who have a solid pipeline have an amazing first week from this alone.

This is not just a weekly, but a daily high-touch process that we've used to scale corporate sales teams to 8 and even 9 figures, and small mom-and-pop businesses to 7 or 8 figures.

If at any point you have a question, an issue with a salesperson, or you need to convey a change that your salespeople need to know, you'll speak directly to your account manager. You won't even need to speak to your sales team if you don't want to. Once you speak to your account manager, we will immediately work with your sales team to relay your information, correct the problem, or do whatever needs to be done. And we'll do it in a way that gets the most out of your salespeople using our proven management process.

Once you finish your ***How It Works Pitch***, the next thing you should ask is simply *"Do you have any questions?"* At this point, they will likely ask multiple questions about your offer to gain clarity on how it works, what the results could be, etc. You'll go ahead and answer those questions, and if you hear an objection, you will handle it.

Do not volunteer any more information than what they ask. If you start talking about all the features of your program, you can kill the sale with information overload and talk about things they don't want. Stick to what they ask.

Eventually, you'll get to the magic question …

PHASE 12: PRICE

In this final phase, we deal with the biggest hurdle of all. **Price.**

How much is it?

It's important to never volunteer or even talk about price until they ask. Keep answering questions until they ask about the price. If they do not ask about the price after several rounds of questions, then simply keep saying, *"Do you have any other questions about how to get started?"*

They will inevitably ask for the price. It's very important that they ask for the price and you don't volunteer it.

You want to make sure you retain control of the call, and when you volunteer the price without being asked, you lose that control.

If they are already aware of the price, this makes it even easier because you can simply ask, *"When would you like to schedule your onboarding call? Great. What kind of card will you be using today?"*

You would be surprised how many people will just whip out their card and start reading off the numbers. However, if they are not aware of the price, you'll need to state it in a way that's super simple, such as, *"The investment is $5,000."*

Once you announce the price, you need to SHUT UP. Do not open your mouth. I don't care if the building starts burning down around you, you keep your mouth closed until they speak. Sometimes this will be as long as 1-2 minutes of silence. Do not speak until they speak. If you speak first, you will most likely lose the sale. Do not speak. I cannot reiterate this enough. This is the most important part of this process. **DO NOT SPEAK.**

I remember one time a prospect talked to themselves for over 100 seconds straight. They went from, *"I can't afford this"* to *"But I can't afford NOT to do this"* all on their own within about a minute and a half, without me speaking. The next thing they said was, *"Do you take Mastercard?"*

At this point, you'll either get a sale or a deposit. You might need to schedule a follow-up call or set up a payment plan. Or you'll need to overcome an objection.

THE OBJECTION PHASE

In a perfect world, if this sales script is executed flawlessly, you will get no **Objections**. Or the objections you do get are nothing more than them needing to hear reassurance. But we don't live in a perfect world, and not everyone will execute this script flawlessly every time. And even if they do, it's always possible the prospect will have a hang-up and need to talk it out.

So when that happens, it's time to overcome objections. While handling objections is not within the scope of this booklet, I will go ahead and give you a few quick ways to handle some common objections in case you have yet to order the *Pocket Guide to Handling Sales Objections*, found at CloseDeals.com/books.

OBJECTION: *I've tried products like this before and they haven't worked, what makes yours any different?*

Most salespeople would respond to this and talk about how great their product is, how many features it has, how many people have gotten results from it, and why it's the best. *That is the absolute worst thing you can do.* If you have done this previously, I can tell you right now **you don't know how to sell.** I don't mean to say that to be harsh, I mean to say that to wake you up but you need to pay attention to the content in this book.

When a prospect asks this, they're not really asking this. What a prospect says and what they are thinking are almost always completely different. In reality, they're thinking of a very specific situation that has already happened in the past when they bought another product and do not want that situation to happen again.

So you have to go after that, and not the question they actually ask. Simply say …

I understand you bought products like this before and they haven't worked, in order for me to best answer your question, can you give me an example of something that happened with a prior product you purchased?

They will proceed to tell you a very specific situation that happened, and if they do not get super specific, then you must push for specifics.

So they may say something like …

Well, I bought this consulting program and it only had one call per month, and I really think I needed more than that.

So now you know that essentially they didn't think they received enough support. If you know your product, and you know the amount of support you give is higher, then it's very easy to close this deal.

For instance, we sold $12 million worth of my ***Digital Millionaire Coaching*** program, and we heard this objection all the time. They would usually tell us that in other programs, they only received one call per week or even only one per month. But we offered four calls per week in our program.

So we would say, *"Do you think if you had one call a week instead of one call a month you would achieve your goals a lot faster?"*

They say YES. So then we say, *"Great! What if you had two calls per week?"*

They say YES YES YES! So we say, *"Well that's great news because we do not have one, not two, not even three but we actually have four calls per week. Do you think if you had four calls per week you would achieve your goal substantially faster than that previous program?"*

They say YES and so we say, *"Well that is the difference between our program and that one."*

What you are doing here is specifically addressing their concern instead of going on and on about your program and all the features they don't care about. That's the worst thing you can do.

Now let's just say for a moment that your program does not offer more support, or has more features, or has a longer length of time, or whatever. Now you can go ahead and objection-handle why they don't need whatever it is they're asking for. But that is a much longer explanation than this one, so I cover how to do that in the objection booklet, which you can get by going to CloseDeals.com/books.

OBJECTION: *I'm on vacation for the next month and can't take advantage of the program until then, so I'll wait till I am back.*

This one is super easy to overcome, especially if you have some sort of coaching program. What they are saying here is a real objection. If you have a six-month coaching program and they're leaving for the next month, they're not going to get an entire month's worth of the service they paid for. They're absolutely right.

So all I used to do is say something like the following …

I understand that you don't want to lose an entire month's worth of the service you're paying for. If you'll go ahead and get enrolled today, I'll add an extra month onto your coaching contract, you can go on vacation, come back and you'll have the exact amount of time you paid for. However, if from now until the time you come back, you decide you want to pop in to the members area, you're free to do so and you can consider that bonus time. Will that work for you?

I can't think of a time this didn't work. This is called the **Bonus Time Close** and it's a form of a **Concession Close**. It's where you give something extra (a concession) to the customer that is of great value to them but doesn't cost you much (if anything at all) to deliver.

OBJECTION: *I want to talk to a client about their results first.*

This objection simply comes down to trust. They're asking this for one of two reasons.

1. Either you have absolutely no client testimonials that you've posted publicly, and if that's the case, then you need to go do that before you start taking sales calls. That's called marketing, and without marketing, it's going to make sales extremely difficult.

2. They don't fully trust the testimonials and results you HAVE posted publicly.

So what I've done in the past is use **The Liar Close:**

I understand you want to talk to our clients, but one thing we don't like to do to our clients is turn them into salespeople. Just like them, I'm sure you're very busy and don't want to be bugged every time we'd like to make a sale. So here's what I'll do. If you'll enroll today, and I'll put this in writing, once you log into the program you can network with our existing clients, including the people you've seen post testimonials. If you find that a single testimonial we posted is inaccurate in any way, I'll not only refund your money but I'll also let you keep the program. Are you opposed to that?

This has always worked for me and I've never had to give a refund. So if you're worried about getting a refund, that probably means you're a liar and your testimonials aren't true. So you better address that before learning to sell! **That's why it's called The Liar Close.**

BONUS: THE POSSESSION CLOSE

Here's a nice bonus close for you. Let's say you've done all this and they're just still on the fence. You can say the following …

I understand you're nervous about making this investment. So here's what I'll do for you. I'll give you a 24-hour pass to fully experience the product before you buy. You can log in, watch the modules, network with the other members, and even make a post that asks if everyone thought their investment was worth it. We will schedule a follow-up call 24 hours from now. On that call, you can decide if you'd like to keep the program or not. If so, we'll process your payment and let you keep access. If not, will revoke access and part as friends. Does that work for you?

I learned this close back when I owned a bar and my girlfriend at the time was a pro bartender. We had shot girls that would try to sell shots but couldn't push them. So she figured out a way to sell out tray after tray. She would walk up to a customer, take out the shot, and hand it to them. Once they took possession of it, she would then say, *"Do you want a shot?" … instead of asking before handing it to them.*

Once the customer took physical possession of the shot, it was a lot harder for them to say no. So they almost always said yes.

This is called **The Possession Close** and years later I used it in my online course business to sell an extra $1 million worth of enrollments per year.

NOTE: If you are worried about the prospect downloading all your content and bailing, that is very unlikely to happen. Especially on 24-hours notice. If you are still worried, then only give them access to a portion of the product, but make it juicy.

BONUS: THE 1 TO 10 CLOSE

Finally, this is my favorite close. I'll give you an example from a recent call I had with a prospect.

Them: *Dan I'm just really nervous that your certified closers won't be able to close as well as the ones I already have.*

Me: *I totally understand. Let me ask you a question. On a scale of 1 to 10, how good do you think you are at teaching someone to sell?*

Them: *Probably two or three. I don't really have much sales training experience.*

Me: *Got it. So with everything you know about me and my company and what we've done in the industry, on a* *scale of 1 to 10, how good do you think we are at teaching people to sell?*

Them: *Well, probably a 9 or 10.*

Me: *Got it. Well, let's say we are an 8 to be conservative. Forgetting the current situation we're talking about, if you were a betting man and you had to put money on whether or not an 8 would outperform a 2 at teaching someone to sell, or for that matter* anything, *who would you bet on?*

Them: *Yeah, I get your point. I would totally bet on you.*

Me: *And you already know that if we make just one extra sale per month, we completely cover our fee AND take the massive burden of managing your sales team off your shoulders. You yourself said that you would bet on us, so the only question is ... Are you knowingly going to make less money? Or are you going to do what you already know you need to do and let us work together to blow up your sales?*

They wired the money 10 minutes later.

Most of the time prospects already deep down know what the right answer is, but they have to work through it. They have to say it out loud. If they don't say it out loud, they can't make a decision. Once they hear themselves say what makes sense, now they can do what makes sense.

The **1 to 10 Close** works best when you have authority in the space and a logical path to the conclusion that they will get the result much easier or faster if they had your help rather than doing it on their own.

AN IMPORTANT NOTE ABOUT MARKETING

Marketing is what makes sales both possible and easier. The better you are at marketing, lead generation, social media content, copywriting, email nurturing, etc., the easier it will be to close the prospect once they actually get on the phone.

If you are generating leads without much credibility, clarity, or authority being presented to the prospect through marketing, the sales call will be extremely challenging.

You can still close the sale, especially if you follow this **Big Money Script**, but in the modern world where people can look you up online in an instant, it's important to have things to show when they do. That said, you can grab ***The Pocket Guide to Online Marketing*** at CloseDeals.com/books if you want to make sure all that is on point.

You can also find tons of free marketing and sales tutorials on my YouTube channel at:

YouTube.com/DanHenry

I used to charge $10,000+ for online courses and coaching (including this script), but since I retired as a consultant, I give all that same information away for free on YouTube. Take advantage of it!

WHAT'S NEXT ...

I sincerely hope you have enjoyed this guide. It took time and effort to make sure I clearly articulated the sales script I've used to completely change my life and over 1,200 of my clients' lives.

In fact, this **Big Money Script** is responsible for creating multiple 7- and 8-figure businesses from scratch—businesses that came to me with literally zero sales to start.

While I have retired from coaching and consulting to focus on bigger ventures, I've tried my very best to give you the proven script for High Ticket Selling in this short pocket guide.

However, what will make this script successful in your company, is not the script itself. <u>It's mastery of the script</u>. Mastery is when you practice something so much that it becomes effortless. It becomes second nature.

At this point, you have two options ...

Option 1: You can read this book 100 times, practice it every day, and over the course of hundreds of sales calls, get better and better and better at it. You can also buy a copy of this pocket guide, give it to everyone on your sales team, and drill them every day on implementing this script.

Option 2: You could have us do it for you. When you sign on with CloseDeals.com, we either build a sales team for you or take over managing your existing one.

In other words, we make sure the people selling your products have mastered and continuously maintain mastery of the script, as well as handling objections, following up, and all the other sales tactics taught in these pocket guides.

And the best part is, we structure our service in a way that it doesn't cost you a dime. We will not only make you far, far, far more money than you would make if you tried this yourself, but we will take that massive burden of doing your own sales calls or constantly managing a sales team off of your shoulders.

But to quantify that in real terms, 100% of our clients cover their monthly investment with us by making one or two extra sales per month. And if you don't believe you will get an extra one or two sales by having us handle your sales team for you, <u>then you should rip this guide up right now and throw it in the trash.</u>

But if you're determined to use this guide and do it yourself, we encourage you to do so! That is, in fact, exactly why we wrote it!

If you use it and it increases your sales, all that we ask is that you share these pocket guides with your peers. **That's how you can become a valued member of #closenation** simply by spreading the word.

And if you're looking for more resources like this pocket guide, simply head over to CloseDeals.com where you can not only access more content but you can also apply to become a high-ticket closer on our team—or even request to have our team implement the **Big Money Script**, overcome objections, and close deals for you.

Remember, the biggest expense in your business is lost sales. If you're tired of missing sales, use this guide religiously.

ABOUT THE AUTHOR

Dan Henry, *Wall Street Journal* bestselling author of *Digital Millionaire Secrets*, is a professional speaker, founder of multiple million-dollar companies including GetClients.com, the CRO and Co-Founder of CloseDeals.com, and one of the most influential entrepreneurs in the world.

Dan started his first company to pay his way through college. His first efforts, while only mildly successful, inspired him to drop out of college and pursue entrepreneurship full time. Since then, Dan has generated over $30M in revenue in his business, which he attributes in part to the Big Money Script found in this book. Dan has even closed over $1 million from stage in a single day using many of the strategies he freely shares on YouTube.

He has grown a massive following and has been featured in *Forbes*, *Entrepreneur Magazine*, *Business Insider*, and more.

Dan is committed to sharing his system with others while also offering sales and closing services for marketers and entrepreneurs. He is the father to Bruce, a beautiful baby boy, who Dan named after his favorite superhero.

NEXT STEPS

Whenever you're ready, here are 4 ways we can help you master YOUR sales process:

1. Have us build or manage your sales team.

If you are interested in having us manage your existing sales team so they consistently maintain a high close rate (or we can build a rockstar team to sell your offers for you), email hello@closedeals.com with "Manage" in the subject line.

2. Learn to become a high ticket closer.

If you are a sales professional who wants to make more money with higher commissions or are new to sales and want to earn 6-figures in commissions (without owning your own product), email hello@closedeals.com with "Closer" in the subject line.

3. Have Dan or Phil Speak at your event.

If you are interested in having myself, Dan Henry, or my partner, Phil Bohol, speak at your event, send an email to business@closedeals.com with "Speaking" in the subject line.

4. Need something else?

Send an email to hello@closedeals.com and let us know how we can help.